17.00
$16.95

DATE			
NOV 2 8 2016			

BAKER & TAYLOR

THE SOUND THAT JAZZ MAKES

Carole Boston
Weatherford

Illustrations by
Eric Velasquez

Walker & Company

New York

This is Africa where rhythm abounds
and music springs from nature sounds,
played on a drum carved from a tree
that grew in a forest of ebony.

This is a kalimba chiming for rain
while a high priest chants the same refrain.
These are the dancers who leap and spin
wearing grass skirts and leopard skin.

This is the pulse of countless hearts
aboard the slave ships chased by sharks;
captives bound for a place unknown
on angry waves in boats that moan.

This is the harbor where slave ships docked
and Africans stood on auction blocks;
human chattel, bought and sold,
traded as if they were silk or gold.

This is the field where slaves turned the soil,
and chanted of freedom while they toiled
to pass the message, through secret codes,
of stealing away on pitch-dark roads.

This is how runaways asked the Lord
to guide them with the drinking gourd,
a compass in the sky at night
leading them onward in their flight.

This is the banjo the farmer plucked
after the corn was picked and shucked
while a young boy clacked a pair of spoons
and folks danced jigs beneath the moon.

These are cakewalkers dressed so fine
bouncing—hop-skip—down the line
to the steady beat of a ragtime tune
filling a honky-tonk saloon.

These are the songs of blood and sweat
of men laying tracks and casting nets,
of the Delta bluesman whose guitar whines,
who howls of heartbreak and hard times.

This is the church where gospel rocked,
with shouts of praise that called the flock
to lift their voices, clap their hands,
and march on toward the Promised Land.

This is the steamboat *Dixie Queen*
that showcased a combo from New Orleans,
where Satchmo learned to blow his horn
and some folks claim that jazz was born.

This is Harlem where Duke was king,
Lady was crowned, and Count ruled swing,
Cab Calloway hollered, "Hi-de-ho!"
and Ella scatted in the spotlight's glow.

This is Birdland where jazz broke free
and the sounds of bebop came to be,
where horn men trumpeted things to come
and gold-toned saxophones blared and hummed.

This is the rapper whose boom box blasts.
These are musicians inspired by the past.
They all hear the age-old, far-off beat
of Africa drumming on every street.

JAZZ is a downbeat born in our nation, chords of struggle and jubilation, bursting forth from hearts set free in notes that echo history.

This is the sound that jazz makes!

In memory of my father, who had an ear for good jazz. —C. B. W.

For my wife, Deborah, and the countless musicians who enrich
our lives every day. —E. V.

The paintings of Ella Fitzgerald, Cab Calloway, Billie Holiday,
Count Basie, and Duke Ellington are based on photographs taken
by William Gottlieb. The painting of John Coltrane is based
on a photograph by Henri Dauman.

Text copyright © 2000 by Carole Boston Weatherford
Illustrations copyright © 2000 by Eric Velasquez

First published in the United States of America in 2000 by Walker Publishing Company, Inc.

Published simultaneously in Canada by Fitzhenry and Whiteside, Markham, Ontario L3R 4T8

Library of Congress Cataloging-in-Publication Data

Weatherford, Carole Boston, 1956-
   The sound that jazz makes / Carole Boston Weatherford ; illustrations by Eric Velasquez.
      p. cm.
   Summary: An illustrated history of the origins and influences of jazz, from Africa to
contemporary America.
    ISBN 0-8027-8720-7— ISBN 0-8027-8721-5 (reinforced)
      1. Jazz—History and criticism—Juvenile literature. [1. Jazz.] I. Velasquez, Eric, ill. II.
Title.

ML3506.W42 2000
781.65′09—dc21   99-055284

Book design by Claire Counihan

Printed in Hong Kong

10 9 8 7 6 5 4 3 2 1